EXCEL CONDITIONAL FORMATTING CHAMPION

(Excel Champions Series)

HENRY E. MEJIA

EXCEL CONDITIONAL FORMATTING CHAMPION

Copyright © 2019 HENRY E. MEJIA

ISBN: 9781795160407

OTHER BOOKS BY HENRY E. MEJIA

GET THE COMPLETE

"EXCEL CHAMPIONS" SERIES

Scan the QR Code or go to
https://bit.ly/hemejia1 to learn more
about "Excel Champions"

CONTENTS

ACKNOWLEDGMENTS

I would like to thank all those who supported me throughout the creation of this book, either with words of encouragement or with ideas to improve it.

INTRODUCTION

Welcome to a new Excel Champions Series book!

What characterizes this series of written courses is that you will learn while you practice because they are full of exercises, examples explained step by step, and real life applicable situations. I also include Excel files so you can practice all the book exercises at home. In fact, you will have 30 exercises to practice with.

Did you know that being an Excel Champion increases your chances of getting promotions and better jobs? If you do not believe me, continue reading.

In fact it is very simple to explain: The person who is an Excel Champion can complete the work better and investing less time in front of the computer, as a result has more time available to tackle other activities that need attention and achieve a better outcome at the end of the day.

I know this because I have personally experienced it. Thanks to Excel I was able to get a better job and also thanks to Excel I was promoted. In case you're thinking about it, it was not in any Business Intelligence department nor in Corporate Finance (where Excel is extremely indispensable), it was in the Accounting department and the Sales department. Why did my bosses give such importance to Excel knowledge?

Actually Excel is used in almost any department of any company, private or government. Wherever you work, being an Excel Champion will give you a clear advantage over your other co-workers and will put you in a position to move up or look for a better place.

HOW CAN THIS BOOK HELP YOU BECOME AN EXCEL CONDITIONAL FORMATTING CHAMPION?

This book was written to teach you quickly and easily the correct way to use the Conditional Format tool.

This book is part of the "Excel Champions" series and is written in a simple and clear language.

If you have ever used graphs in Excel or Power Point you will agree that is better to present data in a visually pleasing way, so that the information is better understood.

With Conditional Format you can highlight quantitative and qualitative data automatically, which will allow you to better communicate your ideas and allow your other colleagues to understand what you are trying to communicate.

It's time to start your journey to become an Excel Conditional Formatting Champion.

GET YOUR 13 PRACTICE SPREADSHEETS (.XLSX)

Before starting Chapter 1, get your 13 practice spreadsheets. To get them immediately just **Scan this QR Code** or **go directly to** https://bit.ly/hemejia2 **and** **follow** **the instructions**

If for any reason both the QR Code and the Link don't work, send an email to ems.online.empire@gmail.com saying: *"Hello, I bought your book EXCEL CONDITIONAL FORMATTING CHAMPION and I need the 13 practice spreadsheets".*

Now, it is time to start Chapter 1. Let's go!

CHAPTER 1:

WHAT IS CONDITIONAL FORMATTING AND WHICH ARE ITS BENEFITS?

In Excel, "formatting" means visually changing a cell. Some examples of format are:

• Center the words

• To align to the right

• Fill the cell with one color

• Underline the words

• Words in bold

• Modify the font color

• Modify the size of the words

Conditionals in Excel are logical sequences that normally follow the pattern "If the CONDITION is met, then Excel FORMATS the cell". Some types of conditions are:

• The value of the cell is lower or higher than other

• The value of one cell is the same as another

• The cell contains a certain letter, word or phrase

• The values are duplicated within a group of several cells

• The values are within a range of dates

• The values are the minimum or maximum values within a group of cells

• Many other conditions can be added

So, to explain it simply, CONDITIONAL FORMAT means to automatically format a cell (with any of the previous formatting options) when the condition we want is fulfilled.

"CONDITIONAL FORMAT means to automatically format a cell when the condition we want is met"

With the conditional formatting tool it is extremely easy to automatically highlight the information that interests you, allowing you to recognize important information for decision making in a matter of seconds.

CONDITIONAL FORMATTING EXAMPLES

EXAMPLE 1: Imagine for a moment that you need to find 10% of the higher values in the following table.

$	12,987	$	10,013	$	15,374	$	17,859	$	15,357
$	21,063	$	21,960	$	24,124	$	16,694	$	20,379
$	24,548	$	27,985	$	18,331	$	20,087	$	20,738
$	16,338	$	12,128	$	14,737	$	29,622	$	22,304
$	13,077	$	18,284	$	17,242	$	25,142	$	21,184
$	26,904	$	22,268	$	29,995	$	23,040	$	14,467
$	10,899	$	11,486	$	17,632	$	18,182	$	14,930
$	24,807	$	23,216	$	10,814	$	23,004	$	28,096
$	13,543	$	22,207	$	25,858	$	16,111	$	17,892
$	28,782	$	14,308	$	17,011	$	26,171	$	13,980
$	19,498	$	24,938	$	21,053	$	24,735	$	20,536
$	15,145	$	20,030	$	29,021	$	20,080	$	11,518
$	23,545	$	26,763	$	25,402	$	10,900	$	21,565

The conditional formatting tool helps you achieve it easily in less than 20 seconds. When you order Excel to find 10% of the higher values and color the cell in green automatically.

In this example, the condition was "10% of the top group values". The group consists of 65 values, 10% is 6.5, so Excel automatically formatted the 6 cells that are the higher.

$	12,987	$	10,013	$	15,374	$	17,859	$	15,357
$	21,063	$	21,960	$	24,124	$	16,694	$	20,379
$	24,548	$	27,985	$	18,331	$	20,087	$	20,738
$	16,338	$	12,128	$	14,737	$	29,622	$	22,304
$	13,077	$	18,284	$	17,242	$	25,142	$	21,184
$	26,904	$	22,268	$	29,995	$	23,040	$	14,467
$	10,899	$	11,486	$	17,632	$	18,182	$	14,930
$	24,807	$	23,216	$	10,814	$	23,004	$	28,096
$	13,543	$	22,207	$	25,858	$	16,111	$	17,892
$	28,782	$	14,308	$	17,011	$	26,171	$	13,980
$	19,498	$	24,938	$	21,053	$	24,735	$	20,536
$	15,145	$	20,030	$	29,021	$	20,080	$	11,518
$	23,545	$	26,763	$	25,402	$	10,900	$	21,565

EXAMPLE 2: Now we have a table with sales, names and brands of mobile phones. You want to find the 20 smallest values.

As I mentioned, with conditional format it is extremely easy to highlight information you need. In the image below you can see that in a matter of seconds you found the 20 smallest values.

	SAMSUNG	NOKIA	LG	SONY	MOTOROLA
Sana	$ 25,182	$15,106	$14,214	$21,754	$ 22,467
Leida	$ 16,480	$22,342	$11,612	$16,884	$ 18,968
Christiane	$ 29,702	$16,465	$13,584	$21,947	$ 25,785
Tonja	$ 13,228	$16,234	$13,451	$13,646	$ 28,438
Rolando	$ 16,312	$16,925	$27,171	$29,930	$ 17,889
Casandra	$ 17,862	$21,929	$16,906	$24,335	$ 27,516
Erik	$ 25,135	$27,831	$17,250	$23,910	$ 24,126
Ezequiel	$ 10,219	$13,363	$18,215	$16,910	$ 25,343
Selena	$ 27,335	$25,834	$23,222	$21,479	$ 20,898
Milly	$ 11,262	$18,933	$19,868	$15,405	$ 12,259
Herminia	$ 20,576	$23,796	$20,746	$22,146	$ 15,732
Juan	$ 15,396	$16,610	$16,251	$13,622	$ 17,499
Niesha	$ 27,445	$18,241	$14,086	$20,714	$ 20,854

The relevant information that you can obtain in this simple example is that:

• Tonja is the one with the most difficulty to sell almost all the brands.

• The brand that sells more easily is Motorola.

That information is very valuable to make decisions. In this simple example you can realize that conditional format is eally useful , now imagine the benefit you can get when you use that same tool for more complex situations.

EXAMPLE 3: Now you have a similar table with the profits per company and you want to know the best ones, the average ones and the worst ones. Also you want to know which year was the best, and you want the information in a simple and visual way.

	A	B	C	D	
2011	$ 26,554	$ 49,876	$ 11,209	$ 32,464	$ 120,103
2012	$ 44,826	$ 17,609	$ 38,542	$ 46,752	$ 147,729
2013	$ 41,809	$ 34,980	$ 35,947	$ 18,187	$ 130,923
2014	$ 13,194	$ 48,279	$ 28,524	$ 23,020	$ 113,017
2015	$ 39,276	$ 29,444	$ 21,095	$ 44,220	$ 134,035
2016	$ 20,459	$ 41,733	$ 35,966	$ 46,671	$ 144,829
2017	$ 18,803	$ 28,459	$ 47,940	$ 16,684	$ 111,886

Notice that in a matter of seconds you can color the values in a degraded way, the one with the darkest color is the highest value, the one with no color is the lowest value, and all the intermediate ones are shown with a color scale .

Additionally to the right is the sum of all of the sales of each year, which includes a bar visually indicating the information in the form of a graph. Those two things can also be done with conditional formatting.

The number of situations in which conditional formatting can be used are a lot and it usually offers a quick and visually comfortable solution to analyze and present information.

QUICK CHAPTER SUMMARY:

• The Conditional Formatting tool is used to format a cell automatically.

• Formatting means changing the shape, color, size or background of a cell or group of cells.

• Conditional format offers a quick and visually comfortable solution to analyze and present information.

CHAPTER 2:

BEGINNING TO BECOME A CONDITIONAL FORMATTING CHAMPION

HOW TO ACTIVATE CONDITIONAL FORMATTING TOOL?

To activate Conditional Formatting you must first select a group of cells. Do you remember the last chapter where I showed you groups of values in the form of tables or columns? **The first step is to SELECT that range of cells that contains the values you want to format.**

The second step is to find the tool within the Excel menu. To find conditional formatting within Excel follow this path:

- Home

- Styles

- Conditional formatting

After selecting the option "Conditional Format" the following menu will be displayed and you can choose any of the options.

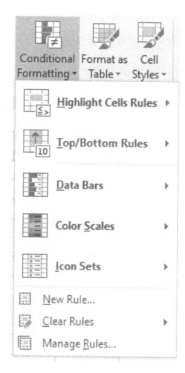

WHICH OPTIONS DO YOU HAVE?

If you look at the menu it has 3 sections that include 8 options in total. These options will be explained in detail in the following chapters but here I explain a quick summary.

1ST SECTION

The first section includes the following 2 options:

- **Highlight Cell Rules:** In my opinion this option has the most flexible conditional formatting tools. You can format a cell based on its value (e.g. if a cell is smaller, equal to or greater than a certain number or a certain cell). You can also format it if it contains a certain letter or phrase at the beginning, middle or end of the text. You can also format a cell in case the value is repeated or in case the value is not repeated. In general, you have many alternatives with this first option.

- **Top/Bottom Rules:** It allows you to identify certain amount of the upper and lower elements. For example you can find the 20 higher or lower values, or you can find 20% of the higher or lower values. Another alternative is to find values that are above or below average.

2nd SECTION

This section includes 3 options:

- **Data Bars:** Data bars were the ones that were used in the last chapter (in the sum of the profits) so you know how they look. According to the value, the bar becomes larger or smaller.
- **Color Scales:** You also saw Color Scales in profits example. You have the option to use scales of 2 or 3 colors.
- **Icon Sets:** You also have a large variety of icons that you can use to identify the

higher, the lower and the average values.

3RD SECTION

When you order Excel to apply a conditional formatting option (from the 1st or 2nd section) to a group of cells, you are creating a new CONDITIONAL FORMATTING RULE.

The 3rd section focuses on those Rules and you have 3 options:

La 3ra sección se enfoca en esas Reglas y tienes 3 opciones:

- **New Rule:** This option allows you to create your own conditional formatting rules and modify some parameters. The reality is that it is rarely necessary to use something so detailed, but I will also explain it in this book.
- **Clear Rules:** It is the option that allows you to choose which rules to delete, that is, in which cells you no

longer want to use conditional formatting.

- **Manage Rules:** Sometimes you can have several rules in the same group of cells and some of them can block others (e.g. If a rule specifies filling cell with a blue color and the other rule specifies filling it with red color). By managing the rules you can decide which rule is more important. You can also modify parameters.

QUICK CHAPTER SUMMARY:

• The first step in activating conditional formatting is to SELECT the range of cells containing the values to which you wish to format.

• The second step is to display the menu and choose one of the options you have.

• The 1st and 2nd sections contain quick options for creating new conditional formatting rules

- The 3rd section mainly serves to manage, modify and delete the existing rules.

CHAPTER 3:

HIGHLIGHT CELL RULES

The first option we are going to practice will be Highlight Cell Rules. As I said earlier, this option is the one that offers the most flexibility.

The **Highlight Cell Rules** option allows you to fill in a certain color the cell that meets the rule you choose. You can quickly access 7 preset rules:

IMPORTANT NOTE:

In the 1st Section (Highlight and Top / Bottom) Excel allows you to choose a preset format (color). The main formats include green, yellow or red fill.

You can also create your own format (e.g. change the fill color, font size, alignment and font style)

GREATHER THAN

This rule allows Excel to automatically highlight (with the color you want) all the cells that are greater than a value or a cell.

For example, imagine that a table with values from 10,000 to 99,000 is presented, and you need to highlight values above 50,000. In that case you should do the following:

Step 1: Select the group of cells

Step 2: Conditional formatting menu> Greater Than

Step 3: Write the value 50,000

57,630	69,269	27,615	39,585	42,236
51,486	25,259	79,096	64,362	18,667
54,039	66,209	66,988	11,995	24,853
32,186	92,449	22,127	60,799	64,895
16,396	96,627	73,403	67,832	29,019
89,590	73,993	45,284	23,281	19,296
22,405	94,708	24,480	38,707	27,211
12,834	98,366	36,213	49,601	73,539
42,188	36,571	71,712	29,647	94,308

LESS THAN

This rule allows Excel to automatically highlight all cells that are lower than a specific value or a cell.

Now imagine that you need to highlight values below 50,000. In that case you should do the following:

Step 1: Select the group of cells

Step 2: Conditional formatting menu> Less Than

Step 3: Write the value 50,000

57,630	69,269	27,615	39,585	42,236
51,486	25,259	79,096	64,362	18,667
54,039	66,209	66,988	11,995	24,853
32,186	92,449	22,127	60,799	64,895
16,396	96,627	73,403	67,832	29,019
89,590	73,993	45,284	23,281	19,296
22,405	94,708	24,480	38,707	27,211
12,834	98,366	36,213	49,601	73,539
42,188	36,571	71,712	29,647	94,308

BETWEEN

This rule allows Excel to automatically highlight all the cells that are between two values or two cells that you choose.

Now imagine that you need to highlight the values between 20,000 and 50,000. In that case you should enhance the following:

Step 1: Select the group of cells

Step 2: Conditional formatting menu> Between

Step 3: Write the value 20,000 and 50,000

57,630	69,269	27,615	39,585	42,236
51,486	25,259	79,096	64,362	18,667
54,039	66,209	66,988	11,995	24,853
32,186	92,449	22,127	60,799	64,895
16,396	96,627	73,403	67,832	29,019
89,590	73,993	45,284	23,281	19,296
22,405	94,708	24,480	38,707	27,211
12,834	98,366	36,213	49,601	73,539
42,188	36,571	71,712	29,647	94,308

EQUAL TO

This rule allows Excel to automatically

highlight the cells that are equal to a value or another cell that you indicate.

In the example you need to highlight the values that are equal to the blue box. You have 2 options:

• Write 20,000 directly.

• Select the cell. This will cause that in case you change the value of the cell, the rule of conditional format will change.

$	10,000	$	7,000	20000
$	20,000	$	12,000	
$	6,000	$	15,000	
$	5,000	$	19,000	
$	20,000	$	4,000	
$	3,000	$	9,000	

Step 1: Select the group of cells

Step 2: Conditional format menu> Equal to

Step 3: Write the value or cell

A TEXT THAT CONTAINS

This rule allows Excel to automatically highlight the cells that contain the text or number you want. You can even be as specific as choosing if you want the text to be found only in the middle or in the end.

Step 1: Select the group of cells

Step 2: Conditional formatting menu> A text that contains

Step 3: Write the text or number. I wrote the number 2 for this example, that's why the 20,000 and 12,000 values were highlighted, because they include the number 2.

$	10,000	$	7,000
$	20,000	$	12,000
$	6,000	$	15,000
$	5,000	$	19,000
$	20,000	$	4,000
$	3,000	$	9,000

A DATE OCURRING

This rule allows Excel to automatically highlight the cells that are within a certain range of dates that you choose.

You have the following options: Yesterday, Today, tomorrow, the last 7 days, this week, next week, this month, last month, next month.

Step 1: Select the group of cells

Step 2: Conditional formatting menu> A date ocurring

Step 3: Select any of the options

10-jun	15-jun	20-jun
11-jun	16-jun	21-jun
12-jun	17-jun	22-jun
13-jun	18-jun	23-jun
14-jun	19-jun	24-jun

DUPLICATE VALUES

This rule allows Excel to automatically highlight the cells that are repeated within a group. Also, by contrast, you can fill in the cells that are NOT repeated, that is, the unique values.

Step 1: Select the group of cells

Step 2: Conditional formatting menu> Duplicate Values

$	10,000	$	7,000
$	20,000	$	12,000
$	6,000	$	15,000
$	5,000	$	19,000
$	20,000	$	4,000
$	3,000	$	9,000

MORE RULES

The option "More Rules" allows you to use conditional formatting with other variants such as:

• Empty cells

• Full cells

- Cells with errors

- Cells without errors

EXERCISES:

It's time to practice, the exercise files includes the answer sheet in the last tab of the file.

The exercises are:

Chapter3ex1

Chapter3ex2

Chapter3ex3

Chapter3ex4

Chapter3ex5

QUICK CHAPTER SUMMARY:

- The Highlight Cell Rules option has 7 quick rules that you can use and it is the most flexible and used.

- You also have the option to create your custom rule

- You can choose the format you want using the "Custom Format" option

Are you enjoying this book?

Do you think it's easy to understand?

Have the exercises helped you learn faster?

Without knowing your opinion I won't know if the book has helped you to become a better Conditional Formatting user.

You can share your thoughts with me by simply writing a **Review on Amazon**.

CHAPTER 4

TOP/BOTTOM RULES

The **Top / Bottom Rules** option includes 6 quick access rules that you can use to identify the lower and upper values quickly and visibly.

You can also customize the format as you wish or use the pre-established formats by Excel.

TOP 10 ITEMS

The "Top 10 Items" option is used to automatically highlight the cells with the 10 highest values. However, when selecting the rule you have the option to choose the number of values you want to fill.

In other words, if you want you can search for the 5 higher values or the 50 higher values. You choose the amount.

TOP 10%

It works almost like the "Top 10 Items". In this case you can apply conditional format to 10% of the highest values.

It is not mandatory to choose the 10%. You can choose to highlight 20%, 5% or the percentage you want.

For example, if you have 60 values and you want to fill the top 5%, conditional formatting will be applied to the 3 higher values (5% of 60 values is 3).

BOTTOM 10 ITEMS

It works in exactly the same way as "Top 10 Items", with the difference that this rule highlights the 10 lower values, or the amount of values that you choose.

BOTTOM 10%

It works in exactly the same way as "Top 10%", with the difference that this rule highlights 10% of the lower values, or the percentage of values that you choose.

ABOVE AVERAGE

This rule is very useful because it performs 2 functions at the same time. First calculate the average of the group of cells you have chosen, and second apply conditional formatting to the cells that are above that average.

Any modification of the values in the group of cells will automatically modify the average.

BELOW AVERAGE

This rule first calculates the average of the values of the group of cells you have chosen and then applies conditional formatting to the values that are below the average.

Any modification of the values in the group of cells will automatically modify the average.

EXERCISES

It's time for you to practice with the exercise files:

Chapter4ex1

Chapter4ex2

QUICK CHAPTER SUMMARY:

• Top / Bottom Rules are the way to quickly and visually identify higher or lower values.

• You can identify any number of values

• You can identify any percentage

• You can identify the values above or below the average

CHAPTER 5

EDIT, MANAGE AND CLEAR RULES

To edit, manage or delete existing conditional formatting rules you must follow a few simple steps.

EDIT RULES

Imagine that you have a table like this one, where the conditional format fills the top 10 values green. Now it's time to edit that rule.

9,608	6,138	3,808	3,971	8,314
5,587	2,724	5,369	4,866	1,730
4,499	7,719	5,113	4,641	2,812
1,442	9,330	4,379	6,783	8,460
7,233	7,844	8,788	1,786	4,052
8,944	9,290	2,322	3,759	1,396
8,354	1,399	2,356	7,770	9,984
1,809	3,122	7,116	8,190	3,906
2,038	4,903	4,862	1,677	5,530

Step 1: Select the group of cells that have conditional formatting> Conditional Formatting Menu> Manage Rules (At the bottom of the menu)

Step 2: Select the current rule and click on "Edit Rule"

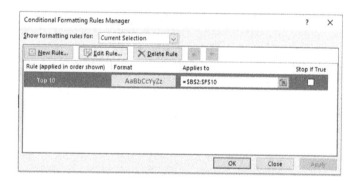

Step 3: You will see a box like this one

below, where you can edit it if you want to apply conditional format to the higher values, lower values, the amount of values you want to highlight or the percentage of values you want to highlight. You can also change to the conditional format of color scale, bars or icons (explained in the following chapters)

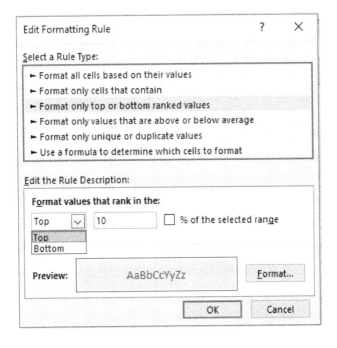

MANAGE RULES

There are times when you have more than

one conditional formatting rule in your Excel file and sometimes the rules are opposed to each other, that is, both conditional formatting rules can apply to the same cell, but it will be highlighted with the color of the Priority Rule .

You can manage the hierarchy of the rules, making some more important than others. In other words, you can order Excel what rule to apply in case two rules are activated in the same cell.

Step 1: Select the group of cells that have a conditional format> Conditional Format Menu> Manage Rules (Down in the menu)

Step 2: Select the rule you wish to prioritize and click on the up arrow. The rule that is at the top will be the most important one.

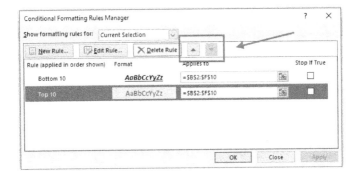

CLEAR RULES

To delete conditional formatting rules you have 3 different options:

• Delete a specific rule.

• Delete rules from a group of cells

• Delete all the rules of the current sheet.

CLEAR A RULE

The process is similar to the one of managing rules, it only differs in the last step:

Conditional format menu> Manage rules>

Select the rule> Click on "Delete Rule"

CLEAR RULES FROM SELECTED CELLS

Step 1: Select the group of cells from which you want to delete conditional format.

Step 2: Conditional Formatting Menu> Clear Rules> Clear rules from selected cells

CLEAR RULES FROM ENTIRE SHEET

Conditional Format Menu> Delete cells> Delete rules from the entire sheet.

QUICK CHAPTER SUMMARY:

• You can edit the conditional formatting rules

• You can change the hierarchy level of each of the rules

• You can clear the rules of a group of cells or the entire sheet.

• You can also delete only one rule, in case you have several of them.

CHAPTER 6

DATA BARS

The second section of the Conditional Formatting menu has 3 options: Data Bars, Color Scales and Icon Sets.

Any one of these 3 options needs to be used with a group of cells, it can not be used with individual cells. The reason of this is because the conditional formatting that is applied to each cell will depend on its size (value) in relation to the others in the group. Now let's get to know the first option: Data Bars

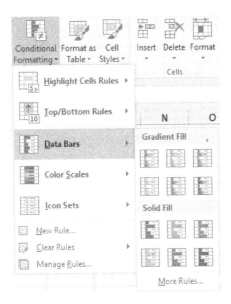

The **Data Bars option creates a mini horizontal bar within each cell of the group**, as if a small mini graphic was formed. The size of the bar varies depending on the value within that cell.

The type of bar can be solid fill or gradient fill. Negative values can also be included, so the bar will grow to the left.

One last important fact is that you can choose between 2 alternatives to configure the minimum of the bars.

The first alternative (which is established by default) keeps the minimum of the bars equal to 0, in other words, for a cell to appear without the bar, its value must be zero.

Here I show you an example where **the bars have a scale from "0" (minimum value by default) to $ 20,000 (maximum value by default).**

$	10,000
$	18,000
$	7,000
$	9,000
$	20,000

The second alternative is to modify the configuration and establish the minimum of the bars (cell without bar) to be the smallest value of the group. In this way the difference between the values is observed more easily.

I'm showing you the same previous example, now with the modified minimums. **Now the scale goes from $ 7,000 (the minimum value of the group), which appears without any bar, to $ 20,000 (the**

maximum value by default).

$	10,000
$	18,000
$	7,000
$	9,000
$	20,000

You can observe the two images with the same values, but the second configuration allows you to see the differences easily.

HOW TO CHANGE THE MINIMUM VALUE?

Step 1: Choose the Data Bars you want, the minimum will automatically be 0.

Step 2: Click on the Conditional Formatting menu and click on Manage rules.

Step 3: Select the rule that you have created and click on Modify Rule

Step 4: In the parameter Minimum Value you will find by default the option "Automatic" but you must change it to

"Lowest value". Click on accept and again on accept.

That way you can switch between the way the bars will consider the minimum value. Any of the 2 forms fulfills the objective of displaying the information visually, it only depends on what you prefer.

MORE EXERCISES

It's time to practice with the exercise files:

Chapter6ex1

QUICK CHAPTER SUMMARY:

• Data Bars creates a horizontal bar within the cell, in the form of a mini graphic.

• The higher the value, the more the bar grows to the right.

• Negative values can be included.

• The empty bars can be the values 0 or the minimum values of the group, depending on the configuration you choose.

CHAPTER 7

COLOR SCALES

Color scales are another form of Conditional Format for a group of cells. They are used to identify the highest, lowest and average values.

The main characteristic is that the colors are degraded and mixed in such a way that it is possible to identify (according to the intensity of the color) how high or low the value of a cell is compared to the others.

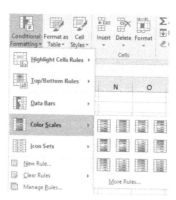

You can choose between two types of color scales:

- The scales of 3 colors

- 2 color scales

3 COLOR SCALES

The higher values are filled automatically with the color you choose. That color is degraded becoming another for values closer to average. And finally the smallest values get another color.

An example of a 3-color scale would be the following:

$	10,000	$	500
$	20,000	$	2,000
$	6,000	$	500
$	6,000	$	2,000
$	20,000	$	1,000
$	1,000	$	300
$	500	$	1,500
$	2,000	$	3,000

2 COLOR SCALES

Similar to the 3-color scale, the 2-color scale assigns a color to the highest values and a color to the lowest values. In the average values, a mixture of both colors is created.

An example of a 2-color scale would be the following:

$	10,000	$	500
$	20,000	$	2,000
$	6,000	$	500
$	6,000	$	2,000
$	20,000	$	1,000
$	1,000	$	300
$	500	$	1,500
$	2,000	$	3,000

MINIMUM AND MAXIMUM VALUES CONFIGURATION

Like the Data Bars, the minimum and máximum values of the Color Scales can be configured with the option "Manage Rules"

By default, the minimum and maximum of the color scale is set to be the lowest value and the highest value in the group of cells.

If you select a scale of 2 colors (green and white), no matter how high the values are, the lowest value will be filled in white, because by default Excel considers it as the "minimum" for the color scale.

For example, in this group of numbers the minimum value appears as white fill because Excel considers it as the minimum in its color scale. **In other words, the color scale ranges from $ 15,000 to $ 20,000.**

$ 15,000	$ 16,000	$ 17,000
$ 18,000	$ 19,000	$ 20,000

When modifying (in Manage Rules) the minimum value the color scale may change a bit.

Step 1: Select the group of cells

Step 2: Conditional formatting menu

Step 3: Manage rules

Step 4: Select the rule and click on Edit Rule

Step 5: In minimum values select "Number" and write 0.

Now the color scale looks different because you selected 0 as the minimum value in the color scale. In other words, a number 0 (or close to 0) would be the only one that would be filled with white.

The color scale now ranges from $ 0 to $ 20,000. That is why the six values are filled with a very intense green, because they are very close to the maximum.

$	15,000	$	16,000	$	17,000
$	18,000	$	19,000	$	20,000

MORE EXERCISES

It's time to practice with the exercise files:

Chapter7ex1

Chapter7ex2

QUICK CHAPTER SUMMARY:

• Color scales fill the cell with a gradient color, depending on the cell value.

• There are scales of 2 and 3 colors

• The minimum and maximum of the color scale can be configured.

CHAPTER 8

ICON SETS

Icon sets are another way to visualize information. The alternatives include:

• Directional icons

• Shape icons (which are actually color changes)

• Indicators

• Ratings

In general, you can use the group of icons that you like the most. Directionals and ratings are good for visualizing performance very clearly, while indicators are very explicit and can highlight information quite well.

The most important thing you should understand about the conditional format with icons is that they can be used in two main ways:

• **Group**: Relating values in a group (like color scales).

• **As an indicator:** Establishing parameters (minimum and maximum) in advance to define what is good of what is bad.

USING THEM WITH A GROUP

Let's see an example of group use. The following table shows the sales of one year. If you select all the values and apply the conditional formatting you want (in this example I use the directional of 3 arrows), you would get something like that.

	SALES	
A	⬇	$ 10,000
B	⬆	$ 17,000
C	⬇	$ 9,000
D	⬇	$ 6,000
E	⬆	$ 20,000
F	➡	$ 13,000

What does that mean? It means that within the group products B and E performed well, product F had an average performance and products A, C and D had a bad performance, but is it really true? Lets see.

The scale that Excel used was automatically created, **from the minimum value of the group to the maximum value of the group, from $ 6,000 to $ 20,000**, in other words, the scale measures $ 14,000 in distance. That scale of $ 14,000 automatically divides Excel into 3 parts: the results in the first third of the scale were shown as a por performance, those in the second third as a neutral performance and those in the third as good one.

USO COMO INDICADOR

Now let's look at the same example but using them as Indicators, explaining in advance to Excel what should be considered as "good", as "neutral" and as "bad".

Suppose the company decides that the minimum acceptable value is a sales amount of $ 15,000, and that a good result would be starting at $ 18,000. How do we order that to Excel?

Step 1: Select the group of cells to which you want to add the icons.

Step 2: Conditional formatting> Icon Sets> More Rules

Step 3: Select the Icon Style (In this case it's the 3 arrows)

Step 4: In Type select Number

Step 5: For the "up arrow" icon write the parameter that the company considers a good result, $ 18,000.

Step 6: For the "neutral arrow" icon write the minimum acceptable parameter for the company, $ 15,000, and click OK.

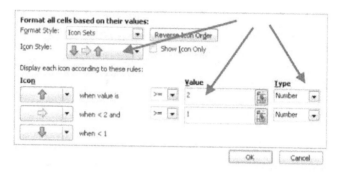

What happens when you do that?

	SALES	
A	⬇ $	10,000
B	⇨ $	17,000
C	⬇ $	9,000
D	⬇ $	6,000
E	⬆ $	20,000
F	⬇ $	13,000

You can see that now only 1 good result is shown, 1 neutral result and 4 bad results. **This happened because you added parameters of what Excel should consider "good" and "bad"**, that way you can get more reliable visual information.

In the first example, 2 good results were shown, 1 neutral and 3 bad results because Excel only compared the values between the group without anyone indicating it what level of sales was the goal.

You can use the same procedure for any of the Icon Sets, just remember to decide if you want to use it in group or as indicator.

MORE EXERCISES

Now yo need to practice with the exercise files:

Chapter8ex1

Chapter8ex2

QUICK CHAPTER SUMMARY:

• Icon Sets work similarly to the color scale, but the icons are easier to recognize visually

• You can use them in groups

• You can use them as an indicator

• To use them as an indicator you need to go first to the "Icon Sets" option and then "More Rules"

CHAPTER 9

FORMAT CELLS WITH A FORMULA

The next step is to have Excel add conditional formatting following a formula that you created specifically for that data group.

The formulas that can be used are many, however the most common use for conditional formatting with formulas is to look for values (high or low) with mobile (or relative) references.

SEEKING HIGH OR LOW VALUES WITH RELATIVE REFERENCES

In the previous chapters you learned how to highlight the cells that contained a greater or lesser value than a fixed number or a fixed cell, but when you want the conditional format to be "mobile" you need to use the custom formula.

When you want cell E6 to decide whether to apply conditional format based on cell D6, but at the same time you want cell E7 to decide based on cell D7, you can choose to apply conditional format one cell at a time (which is very slow) or use a formula for the entire data group.

	D	E
6	$ 85,395	$ 81,970
7	$ 71,323	$ 20,578
8	$ 3,602	$ 72,928
9	$ 69,478	$ 12,602
10	$ 55,175	$ 66,119
11	$ 6,681	$ 6,639

Suppose you want each cell in column E to be highlighted red if it is larger than the data to its left in cell D. You would do the following:

Step 1: Select the group of cells from E6 to E11 (only column E) without selecting any data from column D.

Step 2: Conditional formatting> Highlight Cell Rules> More Rules

Step 3: Select the "Use a formula to determine which cells to format"

New Formatting Rule   ?   ✕

Select a Rule Type:

► Format all cells based on their values
► Format only cells that contain
► Format only top or bottom ranked values
► Format only values that are above or below average
► Format only unique or duplicate values
► Use a formula to determine which cells to format

Edit the Rule Description:

Format values where this formula is true:

| |

Preview: AaBbCcYyZz   Format...

OK   Cancel

Step 4: Write **=E6>D6**

Why that formula? Having selected from E6 to E11, that formula (without Absolute References with signs of $$) tells Excel that

E6 will be subordinated to D6 to make a decision, but at the same time E7 is subordinated to D7, E8 is subordinated to D8 , and thus all the group that you have selected.

Step 5: Choose the Format (color) you want, in this case red is by default

Step 6: OK

	D	E
6	$ 85,395	$ 81,970
7	$ 71,323	$ 20,578
8	$ 3,602	$ 72,928
9	$ 69,478	$ 12,602
10	$ 55,175	$ 66,119
11	$ 6,681	$ 6,639

In this case, you will see that the data in column E was based on the data in column D and the 2 cells that were greater than those on the left were highlighted.

The process is the same for relative (mobile) references of higher, lower or equal values, the only thing that changes are the symbols:

- =E6>D6

- =E6<D6

- =E6=D6

MORE EXERCISES

Now yo need to practice with the exercise files:

Chapter8ex1

QUICK CHAPTER SUMMARY:

• The formulas are used in conditional format mainly to create "mobile" references on which the format decision is based.

• The most common are the greater than , lesser than or equal to.

CONGRATULATIONS!

If you have completed the chapters and the exercises, you can now use Conditional Formatting like a champion!

Because of your dedication, **I decided to share with you the first chapter of my book EXCEL VLOOKUP CHAMPION**, which you will find on the next page.

Also, in chapter 11 I have included several tips that I consider important in your growth as an Excel Champion.

CHAPTER 10

EXCEL VLOOKUP CHAMPION FRAGMENT

As a Bonus and Free Gift, you are getting the 1st Chapter of my book "Excel Vlookup Champion".

If you want to, you can visit the full book on Amazon

WHAT IS A FUNCTION?

An Excel function is a tool used to make calculations, searches, changes or logical reasoning with the data you provide, with the objective of returning a result.

Functions (or formulas) always start with the sign of =

Every time you try to write a function you must select the cell and start with a =

In a simple way, using functions saves you the hard work and it is Excel who works hard to give you the result you are looking for. Less work for you and less time in the office!

"Using functions (formulas) saves you a lot of hard work."

Excel is one of the most powerful software, it has many functions and many tools, and in this book you will learn one of the most useful: VLOOKUP

WHAT IS VLOOKUP?

Vlookup is one of the most useful Excel functions. You can use it in different ways but **basically it helps you find information within a giant amount of data.**

IMPORTANT NOTE:

VLOOKUP is the formula in English.

If you use Excel in Spanish, the formula works the same, with the only difference that VLOOKUP in Spanish is called BUSCARV.

You only need to enter in the formula =BUSCARV instead of =VLOOKUP and voila, everything else remains the same.

Sometimes, you need to find the exact price (or any other information) of a certain Product ID, but you have many products. What someone who is not a Vlookup Champion does is to search the price of each product in their database and copy it manually, one by one. What a waste of time! What a Vlookup Champion does is to use the formula to get the right prices from the database and in 30 seconds all the prices along with their respective Product ID are in place, with zero errors.

If you have a list of names or numbers and you need to relate it to other data, Vlookup helps you find that information in a database, in just a few seconds and without errors

It is possible that you have a list of students, clients, stores, employees, vehicles, invoices, and you need to place certain information next to them without errors to be able to do an analysis with or without graphs, VLOOKUP helps you to do that in a matter of seconds.

EXAMPLE:

Imagine that you have this daily sales table, and you need to fill out the product description and the employee who sold it:

PRODUCT ID	EMPLOYEE ID	PRODUCT DESCRIPTION	EMPLOYEE NAME
4	111		
5	110		
1	110		
3	113		
1	112		
1	111		
2	111		

It would take you easily 3 or 4 minutes to fill it out manually and with the risk of having errors, and there are only 7 sales. When you face hundreds of sales you can end up with some complications. But if you have previously a "master table" where you have the list of all the product IDs and their descriptions **(that "master table" is called Database** and it is usually obtained from the ERP System of the business) you can use Vlookup and within 15 seconds you will have the product descriptions in order. Another 15 seconds and you would have the names of the employees too.

When you are a Vlookup Champion you need only 1 minute to search and write what used to take you 10 minutes without Vlookup

THE BENEFITS OF USING VLOOKUP AS A CHAMPION

Well, it's obvious that knowing how to use Vlookup doesn't make you look sexier in the office (although sometimes it does) but it has many other benefits:

• You can save a lot of time of searching and filling spreadsheets with information of databases. That is, you have more chances to leave the office early and have done what they ask.

• Most of the time you will have zero errors, and when you have one you can immediately notice it. Never again give incorrect information to the boss. Avoid ending up the day with a long face.

• Vlookup makes it easy for you to learn other Excel functions. Combining functions is one way to get the best out of Excel, and using Vlookup as a Champion is a great start to achieve that.

• You can spend more time analyzing the information and searching ways to improve your work. How on earth can you analyze the information if you use hours to obtain it and organize it? By the time you finish you are tired, stressed and hungry! It's better to use VLOOKUP.

Now that you understand the benefits of being a Vlookup Champion, you will be more motivated to be one. In the next chapter you will learn the parts that make up the Vlookup function quickly and easily. Once you understand the structure and its parts you will begin with the exercises.

QUICK CHAPTER SUMMARY

• Vlookup will save you time and prevent you from making mistakes.

Vlookup will allow you to analyze more information and make better decisions in your job or business.

CHAPTER 11

QUICK FINAL EXCEL TIPS

This book wouldn't be complete without a series of final recommendations that can help you to be not only a Conditional Formatting Champion, but also a complete Excel Champion.

Here (in this short chapter) I can't teach you everything I'm going to recommend because they are extensive topics that would not fit in a few pages, it is also information that I teach deeply in other Excel Champions books.

However want to make you the following recommendations with the hope that you recognize the main tools that you must learn to be an Excel Champion.

WHY DO YOU NEED TO LEARN KEYBOARD SHORTCUTS?

First of all I want to recommend that you learn Excel keyboard shortcuts. Keyboard shortcuts are the easiest and fastest way to increase your productivity in Excel. You can easily cut your work time in half.

The reality is that there are more than 100 keyboard shortcuts. My recommendation is that you learn the 10 or 20 main ones. Which are the main ones? The ones you use the most depending the kind of work you have to do in Excel.

Some of those that everybody should use are:

Ctrl + C to copy a cell (with format too)

Ctrl + V to paste the cell that you copied

Ctrl + X to cut the cell (instead of copying it, you remove it from its cell to paste it in another cell)

Ctrl + to insert a column or row (selecting the column or row previously)

Ctrl - to delete a column or row (selecting the column or row previously)

Surely with these shortcuts you can move a little faster. But there are more that are quite useful.

WHY DO YOU NEED TO LEARN VLOOKUP?

The VLOOKUP formula is one of the most used for search and reference in Excel.

When you work with large amounts of data (numerical and text) it is very likely that you have to use the formulas VLOOKUP, IF, MATCH or INDEX.

All these formulas are explained in my Excel Vlookup Champion book, which you can find in the following link: http://bit.ly/VLOOKUPCHAMPION

WHY DO YOU NEED TO LEARN MORE FUNCTIONS?

There are hundreds of functions that can help you to better perform your work, however you may not know them. Sometimes a new function that you learn can save you hours of weekly work in the office.

The important fact to remember about functions is that they tend to relate to each other and become stronger tools when combined or in the form of nested formulas.

I'll give you an example: VLOOKUP. The VLOOKUP function is quite strong and useful on its own, but when you learn to use IF together with VLOOKUP, three things happen:

1) You learned a new function: VLOOKUP

2) You learned a new function: IF

3) You learned a new tool: IF + VLOOKUP

When you learn just two functions you actually have three tools in your toolbox. That is, your tools are not just the number of functions you master, but also include the combinations you can make between those functions.

So the more functions you know, the more combinations you can make and the more chances you have to become an Excel Champion.

WHY DO YOU NEED TO LEARN TO USE CHARTS?

Charts are, by excellence, the way to communicate quantitative information in the business world, in non-profit organizations, in schools, in governmental organizations, in health areas, in sports, etc.

It's very simple, if you want to effectively communicate your numerical data, you need to master the Excel Charts. That includes the use of tables and the correct positioning of them, the selection of the data that you need, the Chart Type selection and the modification of the parameters of the chart.

Additionally it becomes necessary that you learn to discover what a chart wants to "tell you". Correctly analyzing the data in a chart usually leads to better decisions.

If you want to make better decisions in your job or company, it is very likely that becoming an Excel Charts and Graphs Champion will benefit you.

I WOULD LOVE TO READ YOUR COMMENTS

Before you leave I would like to tell you Thank You for buying my book. I hope that the information you obtained in Excel CONDITIONAL FORMATTING CHAMPION helps you in your job or business, and that you can have greater productivity and more free time to use it in the activities that you like the most.

I realize that you could have chosen among several other Excel books but you chose Excel Conditional Formatting Champion and you invested your time and effort. I am honored to have the opportunity to help you.

I'd like to ask you a small favor. **Could you take a minute or two and leave a Review about your experience with Excel**

Conditional Formatting Champion on Amazon?

This feedback will be very appreciated and will help me continue to write more courses that help you and a lot more people.

Share your comments with me and other readers.

ABOUT THE AUTHOR

Henry E. Mejia is an online entrepreneur who discovered the great benefit of knowing how to use Microsoft Excel at an advanced level, and now he devotes part of his time to creating books so that more people can enjoy free time and better opportunities that an Advanced Excel user can have.

Henry also realized that the vast majority of people give away a lot of their life in front of the computer. That time could be used in more productive or more enjoyable activities, only if people knew how to use Excel a little better.

The goal of Henry's books is to open the door for workers and business owners to use Excel more efficiently, so they can have more and better growth opportunities.